MW00913177

SPIRITUALITY AND COMPETITION

STAYING TRUE TO YOUR VALUES

LEWIS M. ANDREWS, PH.D.

HAZELDEN®

Hazelden Educational Materials
Center City, Minnesota 55012-0176

ISBN: 1-56838-004-6

Editor's note:
Hazelden Educational Materials offers a variety of information on chemical dependency and related areas. Our publications do not necessarily represent Hazelden's programs, nor do they officially speak for any Twelve Step organization.

The typeface used in this booklet is Adobe Garamond.

Businessman Jack Stack was asked the secret to his success in turning Springfield Re-Manufacturing from a failing and demoralized maker of heavy-duty engines to one of the most agile corporations in America. He answered with a grin: "Irish Catholic guilt and a brief time in a seminary."

When the legendary coach Vince Lombardi was asked the secret to his success in building a winning team, he replied that he demanded three loyalties of his players: "To God, to country, and to the Green Bay Packers—and in that order."

Most of my professional life has been in education and publishing. I am a research psychologist by training, and I have written mostly on topics in psychology and philosophy.

But six years ago, when my uncle Richard died unexpectedly, I was suddenly plunged into the unfamiliar world of business. My uncle had run the Sieg Corporation, a one-time iron ore and buggy whip distributor, built by my grandfather and his friends into one of America's oldest and largest

1

independent auto parts wholesalers. Over the years, I had inherited a small stake in the company.

Shortly after my uncle's death, it was discovered that the company had problems which were not generally known. Dividends and growth had stopped, and there was a great deal of squabbling among the shareholders, including everyone from distant relatives to former employees. What I knew about auto parts could have fit on the head of a pin, but if writing about psychology had taught me anything, it was the importance of bringing people together. Over time I earned enough people's confidence to be elected chairman of the board.

Over the last five years, I have divided my time between this company and writing and promoting books.

In theory, it would seem I am splitting my professional life into two very different worlds, yet there is one thing they have in common: *they involve competition.* Whether I am selling exhaust pipes or essays on emotional well-being, I am competing against others in an effort to sell the best product possible...at a reasonable price...to the largest possible number of customers.

Having reflected on competition from different perspectives, I've been struck by a paradox. On one hand, virtually everyone who works, no matter what the job, is interested in competition. People in business and professional sports would seem to have the greatest interest in how to perform against competitors, but we all compete—writers for readers, therapists for patients, lawyers for clients, politicians for supporters, professors for research and the esteem of their colleagues.

At the same time that we're interested in competition, we tend to regard it as a negative character trait, especially from a moral or spiritual point of view. The most ambitious character in movies or television dramas usually turns out to be the villain, and the most successful character—especially if he or she is in business—is portrayed as a greedy, self-centered schemer who will stop at nothing to succeed.

Even self-help books on competitive skills reinforce negative stereotypes: *Winning through*

Intimidation, The Leadership Secrets of Atilla the Hun, Confessions of an S.O.B., and *Swim with the Sharks without Being Eaten Alive.*

This unflattering view of competition has a historical basis. Ever since ancient times, writers and teachers have viewed commercial activity as what a modern economist would call a "zero-sum" game. That is, the wealth in the world is seen as a fixed, inflexible amount—so much gold, so many crops, so many horses and cows. Even a hardworking person who has accumulated extra coins or farm animals is suspected of having "taken something away" from neighbors. By extension, very industrious people who have accumulated a great deal of anything are assumed to have gained their wealth in some unethical way.

In truth *wealth* means many things—education as well as money, convenience as well as possessions—and accumulation of it is not a zero-sum game. Yet the myth persists that a competitive person is necessarily bad—and, conversely, that a moral or spiritual person is unconcerned with achievement. Indeed the word *competitive* has taken on a negative connotation when applied to individuals; a competitive business may be viewed favorably, but a competitive person is not to be trusted.

One sad result is that some potentially successful people do not compete at all. The fear of being "too competitive" or "getting caught up in the rat race" becomes a self-imposed prohibition against expressing natural enthusiasm and taking healthy pride in one's talents.

Even people who have achieved personal success in spite of the negative connotations of *competition* may be inhibited by needless guilt and defensiveness. Worse still, they may accept the mistaken idea that being competitive and having character are mutually exclusive. It is this either/or fallacy that can lead people to think they must choose between "right" and "wrong," that is, between ethics and success.

Competition is one of life's greatest opportunities to grow spiritually. But to fully benefit from it, we must gain deeper insight into the true nature of competition—what it is and, just as important, what it is not.

SUCCESSFUL COMPETITION BEGINS WITH TOLERANCE AND UNDERSTANDING

Nearly eighty years ago a prominent turn-of-the-century clergyman and educator, Russell Conwell, wrote a little book called *Acres of Diamonds*. In it Conwell tells the true story of a poor boy from New York City who set out to establish a small do-it-yourself clothing stand, spending his total savings of $1.50 to stock it. Determined to "beat out" the other neighborhood shops, he canvassed the competition, and then invested 87.5¢ to purchase wholesale the needles, threads, and buttons he thought would beat his rivals.

To the boy's amazement, no one would buy any of the goods he had for sale. Though the thread was of finest quality, the needles were straight and sturdy, and the buttons shined, nothing moved. Indeed, he took a dead loss on his entire investment.

Fortunately, the boy was smart enough to strike up conversations with the uninterested customers; he listened long enough to discover exactly what they were looking for—the kind of needles, the color of thread, the size and shape of the buttons. Mustering courage, the boy spent his remaining 62.5¢ buying the kinds of items the customers said *they* wanted. Within days he had the beginnings of a shop that ultimately became one of New York's largest department stores. As the business grew and required more employees, he was careful to hire people who were less concerned with beating up on competition and more willing to listen carefully to customers.

When we set out to achieve something, we make a grave mistake if we focus on our competitors rather than our customers. Our competitive instinct gets turned into an act of war…and yields about as many positive results.

Successful competition means focusing our attention not on the activities of our rivals, but on the needs of our customers. And since meeting the needs of customers has a lot more to do with being attentive and respectful than with being belligerent or heartless, competition really has to do with spiritual values of tolerance and caring.

This is true, Conwell himself observed, whether

the customer we are talking about is someone outside the company who might be in the market for our product or the boss *within* the company who has the power to promote us. In organizations, people get ahead not by stabbing their rivals in the back, but by building confidence and trust in the minds of superiors.

The nineteenth-century German sociologist Georg Simmel, a contemporary of Conwell's, actually compared successful competition to romantic love in his classic book *The Philosophy of Money*. He wrote that normally we think of competition as "poisonous, divisive, and destructive," but in reality, "it achieves what usually only love can do: the divination of the innermost wishes of the other, even before he himself becomes aware of them."

Such "wooing" is not confined to customers, but to everyone involved in the delivery of our product or service. To create and deliver quality products customers want, we must collaborate with co-workers to make it happen. And since getting along with colleagues requires our attention and respect, effective competition comes back to the basic values of tolerance and understanding.

SUCCESSFUL COMPETITION DEPENDS ON HONESTY AND FAIRNESS

Some years ago, I learned of a remarkable Australian organization, the Inter-Church Trade and Industrial Mission (ITIM), and the man who runs it, the Reverend Peter Marshall.

In 1960, representatives from eleven church denominations decided to test the compatibility of spiritual values with real-world competition. They formed a group, mostly ministers, to consult with individuals, businesses, and large agencies about various managerial problems, ranging from how to handle a medical emergency in the mail room to strategic planning for an entire corporation.

"The goal," explained Marshall, "was to provide practical business advice grounded on the spiritual foundation of basic values. One of the points we stressed was that an organization which values integrity above all and pushes the implications of

that as far as it can is really the most competitive."*
The same is true, Marshall hastened to add, for
individuals: *A man or woman who values integrity
above all and who pushes the implications of that as
far as possible within his or her own life is really the
most productive and successful.*

Today, ITIM is one of the most dynamic and
successful consulting firms in Australia. It has
more than 250 chaplains providing guidance to
over 200 companies, many of them internationally
prominent.

In reflecting on the special values which make
for both individual and collective success, Marshall
considers *honesty* critical. It is one of those "front
line expectations people have of each other," he
says. "This is true within organizations, between
buyers and sellers...even in the athletic [arena]."

Once other people come to distrust your word,
everything else begins to disappear—their desire to
work with you, their willingness to rely on you,
their faith in anything you have to produce or

---

* All quotes attributed to Dr. Marshall are from an interview conducted on January 6, 1994.

offer: "It's very simple," says Marshall. "Most people understand it and equate it with your ability to be fair to them. It's not something that really needs to be explained."

And yet the more successful one becomes—the higher one rises or the more aware one is of how a profession really works—the more likely one is to confront some dishonest practice, either within the company or among one's customers. Discovering and coping with dishonesty do not come naturally to many people, because they believe there are only two choices—join the deception or quit. Blowing the whistle, for all practical purposes, is usually just another way to quit.

Marshall himself gives the example of an eager young sales representative for a weekly newspaper. After working very hard, he was promoted to marketing manager. The excitement of the new job lasted only until he discovered that the secret to the paper's success in attracting advertisers lay in inflating circulation figures by 30 percent. If the young man wanted to keep the ad revenues coming in, he would have to collaborate in this pretense. And if his conscience would not let him be dishonest, then it appeared he had no choice but to resign.

When Marshall heard of the new marketing manager's dilemma, he proposed a third alternative the young man hadn't thought of: "Why not see if it's possible to devise a sales strategy that induces advertisers to use your magazine, even if your circulation is not as good as you've claimed in the past? Even if you're not reaching a lot of people, maybe you're reaching the right people for certain advertisers—for example, an upscale apparel store doesn't need to reach everyone, just the people who want a certain kind of clothing. Perhaps it's possible to develop a marketing plan that will enable the newspaper to finally be honest without losing money over the long run."

The point of the story is that the real measure of our integrity, when we face a dishonest situation, is how creatively we respond to that situation. If there is a litmus test of our values in a deceptive environment, it is how sincerely we try to reconcile *our actions* with *our words*, our behavior with what the organization claims to be.

Sometimes we have to face the fact that the situation is probably not going to change for the better, in spite of what we'd like. Perhaps we don't have the authority to do what is necessary...or we can't get the cooperation from higher-ups...or the dishonesty is so endemic that nothing will change it. Then we may have to remove ourselves from the field and find another game to play. But to view this as unfortunate is a little like saying we've missed the opportunity to sail on the *Titanic*, for any competitive organization that is corrupt is inevitably doomed to failure.

Fortunately, we are more likely to discover—as the marketing manager did—that our thoughtful attempts to make the organization succeed honest-ly are well received, often leading to a sigh of relief all around. After all, most people have an intuitive understanding that any achievement built on fraud is standing on a shaky foundation. Deep down, they also know that reconciling words with actions produces a boost in morale that enhances everyone's performance.

THE VALUES THAT MAKE ONE SUCCESSFUL
CAN'T BE FAKED

Is it really necessary to have good values in order to be successful—or just the *appearance* of good values? We've all read the headlines about infamous Wall Street manipulators, people who made millions of dollars by appearing to be honest. Or savings-and-loan executives who made a fortune by sweet-talking small investors and then the government regulators. There's a reason you've heard about these scandals—the people involved are in jail for big-time fraud. Yes, it's possible to be successful in the short run by pretending to have good values, but in the end this kind of manipulation catches up with you—if not economically, then certainly emotionally.

During my high school years I learned that I could get around adult authorities by pretending to be a good student. It seemed that if you got decent grades and flattered your teachers, you could get away with all kinds of things.

On the surface, you might think I got away with it. I was never arrested for any crime and, in fact,

14

ended up at an Ivy League college. Yet psychologically, there was a very real price to pay. I had spent so many years faking a public identity that I'd completely lost touch with my own feelings and sense of direction. For years after, I was plagued by chronic anxiety and bouts of depression, mood swings that began to lift only when I realized the importance of reconciling my words with my deeds. Whatever I had gained materially by "feigning honesty" was more than offset by the aimlessness that comes with sacrificing one's integrity.

What is true on a personal level is also true for organizations. That is to say, we damage ourselves and the institutions we work for by pretending to uphold values that we really don't live by.

Tom Peters, the popular and insightful management consultant, offers corporate and not-for-profit executives many helpful suggestions for pleasing consumers, such as offering consumers 800 numbers for product assistance or drawing upside-down organization charts so that the customer is positioned at the top.

But Peters goes out of his way to say that every

management technique he recommends will backfire unless it goes beyond public relations to reflect some fundamental truth about the company: "The 800 numbers hum only for those who really believe in listening and responding, not those who are merely looking for a PR gimmick.... Draw your organization chart upside down but continue to provide the same careless service, and it won't make an iota of difference—except that you'll become a joke."*

Reverend Marshall recently confided to me the cautionary tale of what happened when his own consulting firm failed to take into account the importance of reconciling image with behavior. An insurance company client needed a new advertising program for selling disability coverage. They built a campaign around the slogan "We Simply Care for You."

But no savvy consumer believed any insurance company really cared for anything, beyond making money. In the case of Marshall's client, nothing in fact had changed except the slogan.

---

* Tom Peters, *A Passion for Excellence* (New York: Warner, 1986), 40.

Eventually the advertising campaign backfired, and the insurance company found itself worse off than when it started.

The solution, Marshall realized, lay in doing something *substantive* to prove the insurance company *actually cared* for its policy holders. As it turned out, this was not all that difficult to do. The insurance company's research showed only 10 percent of all disability claims to be fraudulent. And of that 10 percent, almost all would-be swindlers sought compensation for a period of more than three weeks.

If these statistics were true, Marshall reasoned, why not automatically pay all claims for periods of less than three weeks? This would mean that honest claim seekers would suffer no humiliating questions from suspicious insurance agents or needless payment delays. This policy was implemented, and within months the company's business—and profits—began to grow impressively.

Because the ethical dimension of competition can't be faked, business schools are now paying more attention than ever to values. One of the most innovative and farsighted business programs in the country is taught at the University of St. Thomas in St. Paul, Minnesota. Under the direction of Dr. Kenneth Goodpaster, the graduate faculty do far more than give a single seminar on "business ethics." The cultivation of higher values is a central theme in the introductory management course that all students must take, and the importance of relating ethical judgment to executive decision making is reflected in every departmental offering. One sign of this program's usefulness is that it has attracted an enrollment of *three thousand men and women*, making it one of the largest business schools in the country.

SUCCESSFUL COMPETITION REQUIRES BALANCE

St. Augustine was one of the great guiding figures in the history of Christianity. Augustine lived toward the end of the Roman Empire and remains an intriguing figure to contemporary readers because his early ambitions seem so modern.

He was born near Carthage in North Africa, and his only goal as a young man was to "make it big" by the standards of the day. Augustine had decided that by the time he was thirty he would have a cushy job in the Roman bureaucracy, would be making plenty of money, would be engaged to a wealthy heiress, and would have at least one mistress on the side.

And by the time he was thirty, Augustine had indeed met his goals. He was a professor of rhetoric at the University of Milan, had a hefty income on the side writing speeches for the Emperor, was engaged to a very rich lady from an important Roman family, and also had a mistress on the side.

The only problem from Augustine's point of view was that he was completely miserable. In fact, there is a very moving passage in his autobiography in which he talks about passing a drunken beggar on the street: "For what he had gained with a few coins, obtained by begging...I was going about to reach by painfully twisted and roundabout ways. True joy he had not. But my quest to fulfil my ambitions was much falser."*

It was a short time after this reflection when Augustine experienced his famous spiritual conversion in a garden in Milan; and that's where most people's interest in his story usually ends. The sinners become a saint after all—so it's a happy ending. But I was curious to know what happened to Augustine *after* his conversion. Did this ambitious and energetic man just go off to a monastery and eat vegetables for the rest of his life? Did he really forsake all earthly goals?

What I discovered was that a few months after his conversion, Augustine decided to sail back across the Mediterranean to his native Carthage. He wasn't sure what he was going to do when he got there, but he knew that it was important to temper his goals with a certain kind of integrity.

As soon as he got off the boat, Augustine was recognized as an educated man and was asked to be the acting priest at a local church. This he

---

* From *Confessions*, trans. Henry Chadwick, in Bernard Knox, ed., *The Norton Book of Classical Literature* (New York: Norton, 1993), 849.

agreed to do, as long as he could work according to his values. And he became a priest with such enthusiasm that he was soon made a judge…and after that a bishop…and by the end of his life had become known as one of the greatest educators in the whole of the Roman Empire.

And there is another touching passage in his autobiography when, toward the end of his life, he talks about the importance of having goals and working hard to achieve them. God, he believed, operates through human labor, and the things we build on earth are reflections of a deeper purpose. But Augustine also believed that it was possible for someone to become so narrowly focused on a particular goal—as he himself had done as a younger man—that over time the person completely loses track of his or her real feelings and desires. From Augustine's point of view, it was very important to temper one's goals with certain values, not as a way to stifle one's ambition, but *as a way to know what one's true ambitions really are.*

Dr. Goodpaster makes this same point from a modern perspective. He makes an important distinction between healthy competitive behavior, which is cultivated and improved through a commitment to values, and what he calls *teleopathy*—literally, "goal sickness"—or what Goodpaster calls "the unbalanced pursuit of purpose."*

"While not a physical or mental illness like heart disease or manic depression," Dr. Goodpaster says, the blind pursuit of ambition without any ethical perspective is as self-destructive as any medical malady. Becoming so obsessed with any goal that we begin to ignore ethical considerations ultimately blunts our sensitivity to our real, deeper desires and makes it likely that even the achievement of our conscious purpose will backfire in unforeseen ways or, as in the example of young Augustine, prove strangely unsatisfying.

Regrettably, the line between ethical competition and teleopathy is not always clear...even to people who think of themselves as having good values. This is because all competition requires

---

* All quotations and ideas attributed to Dr. Goodpaster are taken from a telephone interview conducted with the author on February 4, 1994.

disciplined effort over long periods of time, and it is always possible to become so caught up in one's work that what begins with the most honorable intentions develops a life of its own, regardless of any moral or ethical consequences. A closer look at many of the great business scandals in recent years reveals the sad pattern of normally honest and even compassionate executives getting caught up in and eventually brought down by their own tunnel vision.

But such a fall from grace does not happen without warning. Goodpaster has identified three personality traits which help us to know when we may have inadvertently crossed the line from healthy competition to teleopathy.

- *Fixation.* Becoming more focused and concerned about short-term goals than long-term ones; becoming reckless in the pursuit of immediate objectives without fully examining the consequences.
- *Rationalization.* Asking colleagues or subordinates for blind loyalty regardless of the consequences; evaluating some action strictly by

the permissible letter of the law, without regard to the spirit of our actions.

- *Detachment.* Becoming callous to the consequences of one's actions, usually by insisting that the competitive environment is "a jungle," "a rough place," or "an unforgiving world" with no room for compassion, generosity, or genuine feelings.

When we recognize any of these qualities in ourselves, we have the opportunity, as well as the obligation to our long-term competitive success, to stop and give some thought to how we can deliberately cultivate the opposite trait, such as being flexibile when we are fixated, playing devil's advocate when we are rationalizing, doing something for others when we seem detached. From there, we can begin to take an ethical inventory of our behavior. Where have we become excessively judgmental? Are we being dishonest in some important way? Is there any place in our lives where we are violating a value or precept that we have always believed in?

SUCCESSFUL COMPETITION IS SPIRITUAL BECAUSE IT IS INTUITIVE

When we think of how achievement-oriented people go about making important decisions, the descriptive words that usually come to mind are "logical," "practical," or "realistic." It was therefore a real bombshell a few years back when Harvard business professor Daniel Isenberg announced his discovery that the most successful senior managers in American business appeared to disregard almost completely this stereotyped approach to decision making.

For more than two years Isenberg had conducted an in-depth probe into the private thoughts and attitudes of a dozen of the country's most experienced and competent corporate executives. "I conducted intensive interviews," he recalls, "observed them on the job, read documents, talked with their colleagues and, in some cases, subordinates, and engaged them in various exercises in which they recounted their thoughts as they did their work."*

Isenberg spent up to twenty-five days getting to

---

* Personal interview with Dr. Daniel Isenberg, May 26, 1986.

know each manager personally on the job and even read his observations out loud in order to get his subject's reactions.

At the end of his study, Isenberg came to the conclusion that the most important quality successful executives had in common was *their shared ability to hold back on the desire for logical answers to their problems and to let more intuitive solutions percolate up into consciousness*. "I think ambiguity can be destroying, but it can be very helpful to an operation," one of the managers in Isenberg's research confided. "[Ambiguities] yield a certain freedom you need as a chief executive officer not to be nailed down on everything.... The fact is we tie ourselves too much to linear plans, to clear time scales. I like to fuzz up time scales completely."[*]

Indeed, the more Isenberg studied successful managers, the more he found they needed to cultivate intuition in "all phases" of the problem-solving process. He found that successful managers (1) "intuitively sense when a problem exists,"

---

[*] Qtd. in Lewis Andrews, *To Thine Own Self Be True* (New York: Doubleday, 1989), 72.

(2) "rely on intuition to perform well-learned behavior patterns rapidly," (3) "synthesize bits of data and experience into an integrated picture," (4) "use intuition as a check [on] more rational analysis," and (5) "use intuition to bypass in-depth analysis and move rapidly to come up with a plausible solution."*

As it turns out, these high-powered executives were not trading logic for blind impulse. In many cases, these managers use their best rational thinking to sharpen and enlarge their ideas and to explain them to colleagues. What they *were* doing is what all successful competitors do: prevent their desire for logical answers from overriding the deeper wisdom of a good hunch or strong feeling.

Even in the very competitive world of professional sports, we often hear stories of athletes who have excelled in their respective arenas not because of some new technique or the sheer force of willpower, but because they have somehow made the connection between deeper sensitivities and

---

* Andrews, 72-73.

physical prowess. After one of my recent lectures, a young woman in her mid-twenties came up to me and explained how she had finally learned to become a champion at open-water competitive swimming. It seems that a year before, she had contracted an illness which made it necessary to stay out of the water for a few months.

When she was finally well enough to start swimming again, she felt sufficiently out of shape that she decided she would not push herself too hard at her first few meets but would swim "just for the sake of it." She would not even try to think about beating the other contestants but instead "concentrate on the process," sensing her own movement in the water and doing the best she could to "get in the rhythm of a good swim."

To this young swimmer's amazement, the first time she adopted the attitude of swimming well for its own sake, she beat her own record for a mile swim by one minute and fifteen seconds, even coming in ahead of the person who had consistently defeated her in previous meets. Since then, she's been interested in the intuitive side of competition. "I think that's what really makes a difference, not just in swimming but in life," she says.

Now, there are many who will readily agree that successful competition involves a greater reliance on our intuitive powers. Yet they would also argue that having faith in one's intuition is not the same thing as taking a spiritual approach to competition. Perhaps you yourself might be thinking that gambling on a hunch or being true to some deeply felt impulse doesn't have anything to do with God or what churches teach.

But being *spiritual* doesn't necessarily mean we are members of a traditional religion or that we pray in conventional ways. It only means that we are willing to go beyond the materialistic view of humans as mere "biological blobs," chemical machines with no capacity for creativity, freedom of choice, or faith in things unseen. In that sense, intuition and spirituality have a lot in common.

After all, we wouldn't believe in the wisdom of our own intuition if we didn't also believe in our capacity for insight that goes beyond known facts.

We cannot muster the courage to persist in following a hunch that others deride if we don't believe in the power of deeper, nonrational forces.

DON'T UNDERESTIMATE THE VALUE OF PRAYER OR MEDITATION

Some years ago I was asked to give a talk on spiritual values to a group of engineers at the Medtronic Corporation, a very successful high-tech business near Minneapolis.

After the lecture, one of the scientists who had invited me to speak asked me if I would like to see the "heart" of the company. Since Medtronic specializes in the manufacture of cardiac pacemakers, I thought this was probably the appropriate thing to do and nodded with perplexed enthusiasm. A few minutes later I was being led out the door of the manufacturing facility, where I'd been speaking, toward a large building that looked like an executive office complex.

We entered the ground floor of the building, and I saw on one side what looked like the employee cafeteria. We turned in the opposite direction, however, and my guide led me through a door, where I suddenly found myself gazing at the most unexpected room. It was a beautifully silent place, surrounded by glass shelves holding sacred scriptures from many of the world's religions and containing in the center a comfortably carpeted meditation area.

It was explained to me that I was in the Hermundlie Room, built with revenues from the company's first successful products and dedicated by Chairman Earl Bakken to the memory of his deceased brother, Hermundlie. I also learned that the room was designed as a place where employees of any faith could feel comfortable seeking "deeper guidance" for their personal and professional problems and that it was open for this purpose at any hour of the day.

In the years since my lecture for the Medtronic engineers, I have had the honor of speaking for a number of business-related groups and have discovered in the process that prayer and meditation play a powerful role in the lives of many successful people. I have also encountered people like Jack Falvey, a well-known management consultant, who made a similar observation in his controversial article for the *Wall Street Journal* called "Executives Who Rely on a Very Senior Partner."*

"If 'In God We Trust' is inscribed on the coin and currency we all work for," Falvey says, it is also "inscribed in the minds and hearts of many of our business and professional leaders." Citing examples such as former Secretary of State James Baker and Raytheon president Tom Phillips, as well as the thousands of employees around the country who have quietly formed spiritual study groups at their firms, Falvey makes the point that "total self-reliance is not how things actually work." He adds that prayer as a competitive or management technique "should not be discounted."

Unfortunately, this spiritual fact of workaday life is something that isn't talked about very much—even by the men and women who feel they've gained the most from some kind of

---

* Jack Falvey, "Executives Who Rely on a Very Senior Partner," *Wall Street Journal*, 24 December 1990, sec. A, Op-Ed page.

spiritual practice—because in today's environment its meaning is likely to be misunderstood.

To the many skeptics in our world, the idea of petitioning God for guidance is usually thought to mean that the person who prays or meditates is asking for a particular benefit, such as help in overcoming an illness or getting a material possession, like a car or home. Therefore, one might think that taking a spiritual approach to competition means directing one's thoughts toward getting a specific promotion, raise, or business perk.

The real connection between prayer and achievement is, in many ways, the very opposite of this misconception. Spiritual competitors do not petition God for coveted rewards; on the contrary, they pray to become a selfless vehicle for God's will. "*Thy will,*" as all inspired worshippers say, "*not mine,* be done." It is this willingness to surrender one's own ambition to the service of something greater than oneself which aligns the individual mind and heart with a deeper energy and has the paradoxical effect of making one's actions far more intelligent—and fruitful—than might otherwise be possible.

33

Some years ago I came across a fascinating essay originally published in the *Harvard Business Review* called "Skyhooks" by O. A. Ohmann, a former executive with the Standard Oil Company, which illustrates this point. Ohmann says he began writing "Skyhooks" as an attempt to clarify in his own mind the spiritual foundations of achievement, which often go unreported in the usual self-help books and popular psychology magazines: "Textbooks on the techniques of personnel management [have] mushroomed," he observes. Ohmann says there is "a flood of how to improve yourself books," but most are "manipulative," "superficial," and "futile."[*]

Good executives "have the mental equipment to understand the business and set sound long-term objectives," Ohmann explains, "but the best ones have in addition the philosophical and character values which help them relate to eternal values.... Many great executives I have known have something deep inside that supports them; some-

---

[*] Qtd. in O.A. Ohmann, "Skyhooks," in K. Andrews, ed., *Ethics in Practice* (Boston: Harvard Business School Press, 1989), 58-59.

thing they trust when the going gets tough; something ultimate; something personal; something beyond reason—in short a deep-rooted skyhook which brings them calm and confidence when they stand alone."[*]

THE "PROBLEM" OF WINNING

Of course, the confirmed cynic might concede that while being a successful competitor might mean having certain humane qualities, such as relying on intuition or even prayer or meditation, it's still about winning and wanting to be superior to others. And while it may be smarter to concentrate on pleasing your customers and cooperating with colleagues than on denigrating your rivals, the ultimate goal of competition is to get the jump on other people who offer a similar service or product.

"You can talk all you want about competition bringing people together and requiring us to be sensitive to the needs of others," the cynic would continue. "But in the end, if you're going to have

---

[*] Ohmann, 65.

competition, that means for every winner there's going to be a loser. How can you say competition is a spiritual activity when you're talking about a system in which somebody's got to fail? Are you really going to pretend that competitive people don't secretly wish that their rivals would go belly-up?"

This is an important question, which inevitably confronts anyone attempting to demonstrate the possibilities for reconciling spiritual development and ambition. Perhaps the most thoughtful answer was given by none other than Benjamin Franklin, the great American inventor, businessman, diplomat, and practical philosopher.

The time was 1730 and Franklin was still a struggling young printer in Philadelphia. He had reluctantly accepted the invitation of a rather dry minister to attend a series of sermons on morals but was so put off by the first lecture that he refused to go again. Yet the subject continued to fascinate Franklin.

Some days later, he decided—in what was probably the New World's very first psychology experiment—to make a list of what most people considered to be "the most desirable" character traits, practice them daily, and see what effect they might have on his life. "I made," he wrote, "a little book, in which I allotted a page for each of the virtues...I determined to give a week's strict attention to each...marking every evening the faults of the day."*

Toward the end of his life Franklin wrote an autobiography in which he revealed that it was this experiment—the deliberate attempt to improve his values—which really turned his life around and molded him into the successful person history now remembers. But Franklin was careful to make a point of saying that practicing values as a way to compete in life was not about becoming a saint. In his own mind, he was still the degenerate character he had always been, wishing a pox on his enemies and lusting after their wives. The difference was that he would never consider living out any of these thoughts, because he'd learned enough to

---

* Benjamin Franklin, *The Autobiography* (New York: Collier, 1909), 81.

know that values are not about what you *think* but what you *do*.

We cannot judge the value of any activity by the kind of thoughts which cross our minds while we are engaged in that activity. We would never think to condemn the institution of marriage simply because husbands and wives had occasional thoughts of infidelity. Nor would we dream of doing away with the educational system because teachers might, now and then, entertain the fantasy of throttling their most disruptive students. So why does it make any more sense to condemn competition just because every competitor is tempted from time to time to imagine the defeat of his or her rivals?

The spiritual value of our competitive behavior is not based on the purity of every thought that might occur to us while we are engaged in it, but on the integrity of our actions. Have we sought to understand the needs of our customers? Have we developed a working relationship with our colleagues that enables everyone concerned to work to the best of his or her abilities?

Perhaps if there were some indication that being competitive made our thinking worse, made us more selfish or turned us into hypocrites who only pretended to care about the welfare of others, there would be some cause for concern. But studies show us that the more people compete, the more they experience personal success; and the more successful people feel, the more likely they are to want to be generous, both on and off the job. Indeed, the willingness to serve as a mentor and provide helpful guidance to subordinates is almost directly proportional to the level of one's own achievements.

DESTROYING OR DIVERSIFYING?

Still, the stubborn cynic would argue that anyone who is engaged in competitive behavior, however benign it may appear, becomes the willing participant in an economic system in which there must inevitably be losers: small-business people who go broke because they cannot make products as well or as cheaply as another shop down the block, workers who get sacked because their performance reviews are not as good as their colleagues', consultants who lose their clients when times are tight or when another person comes along with a more appealing service. How can we possibly say that our being competitive is an ethical activity when the very fact of our success means that, sooner or later, someone else will fail?

On the surface, this appears to be a legitimate question, and indeed, it has agonized many social reformers down through the centuries who have never been quite comfortable reconciling the social benefits of competition with the reality that in a competitive society some people will fail. But acknowledging failure in a competitive system is not the same as saying that our personal willingness to compete *causes* others to fail.

The problem is that old "zero-sum" argument, which says that there can only be a fixed number of goodies, so that every gain on our part necessarily comes at someone else's expense. In fact, competition increases the number of products and services available to everyone. Our willingness to collaborate with co-workers to provide the best possible product or service at a reasonable price makes it possible for all consumers to better afford what we make and therefore have more left over to buy what other people make as well.

Even our rivals can benefit from our competitive behavior, for in the process of attempting to serve our customers we discover that different consumers have different needs. Some customers like ice cream, for example, while others like frozen yogurt or soft custard. And even within the group of people who like ice cream, there are those who prefer vanilla and chocolate, and others who'd rather go for some exotic gourmet concoction. Inevitably we begin to specialize on the needs of the customers that we feel we can serve best, leaving our rivals to try to please people with different tastes.

Not long ago, our auto parts company tried to measure our success strictly on how much business we could take away from our rivals. We kept lowering prices, attempting to gain a greater market share, and our rivals did the same. Pretty soon nobody was making any money, and customers were complaining about the poor service.

Finally, we realized we had lost track of the real meaning of competition. We needed to focus on the segment of the market we could serve most effectively.

It was only a few months and our fortunes began to turn. We were able to sell more and make a decent profit. Other companies in our line of business also began to do better, especially those smart enough to concentrate on serving the market where they functioned best.

LOSING OR SOUL-SEARCHING?

Does our competitive behavior ever cause a problem for someone else? Yes—in the sense that it inevitably forces that person to act with a greater degree of self-honesty. For if we are succeeding because we have found a better way to make our customers happy, then a rival who feels threatened must ask, "What can I do to better serve my own customers?"

But in thinking about how to be more competitive, our rival may be forced to a deeper kind of soul-searching: Am I in the right job or business?

Is there some other profession or work that would be a truer expression of my interests and intuitive desires? There are some who might say that our competitive behavior has caused this rival to "fail," but the long-term result of our enforced soul-searching is quite often very positive.

Some years ago I knew a man who worked as a dispatcher in a message and package delivery service. He confided to me that when he had first started this job, the company had little competition and he was frequently able to slack off without having to worry. Then a rival firm started up across town, and in order to stay in business, the boss required all his employees to use their time more effectively.

As my friend got more in touch with what it meant to be a good dispatcher, he gradually came to see there was little about the job that appealed to him. He went back to school in an area that interested him, and now works with a large charity, working harder than he ever did as a dispatcher but enjoying it more.

Of course, it is not just our rivals who are forced

by competition to reconcile their work lives with their heartfelt sense of direction. All of us reach points in our own careers where we have to ask ourselves if we are in the right place, if being good at what we do is the same as being true to our innermost needs. Indeed, one of the striking things about people who have developed an outstanding record of achievement in any field is the number of job changes they have had to make before they finally reached a place where their inner lives seemed to match their outer responsibilities.

And even people who have found the right fit discover that it does not last forever. If we are living with integrity, pursuing the goals that emerge from ethical and spiritual discipline, we will find that our inner needs change over time—that to continue to be true to ourselves in the world we must seek out new opportunities for excellence. Sometimes this means taking a new job within the organization where we already work. Other times it means getting involved with a community activity, such as a charity or political group, during our off hours. And for many there comes a time when we must make a radical change of career, pursuing an occupation entirely different from what we are used to.

Competition can be an ethical exercise, a mechanism for helping us to discover who we really are and to find a means for expressing our individuality within the world of work.

Failure is not a pleasant experience. But it does suggest that the most worrisome aspect of failure is not that it is forced by competition with others, but that we resist facing our responsibility to ourselves until circumstances conspire to produce a rude awakening.

Through our failures, we learn the necessity of being true to ourselves, to what we feel and what we know. And by practicing the values that make success possible, we not only contribute to the material abundance of society, but we enable the outward expression of our deepest self.

Dr. Andrews can be contacted at
P. O. Box 459
Redding Ridge, CT 06876